HOME LIFE IN INDIA

HOME LIFE IN INDIA

JOHN FINNEMORE

GYAN

Published by

Gyan Publishing House
5, Ansari Road
Daryaganj, New Delhi-110002
Phone: 011-47034999, 9811692060
E-mail: books@gyanbooks.com

Distribution Network
gyanbooks.com
India, USA, Canada, UK, Australia, France

ISBN: 978-81-212-9346-4 (PB)
First Published, 1917

2nd Impression 2023

Printed at: Gyan Press, Delhi.

HOME LIFE IN INDIA
AUTHOR: JOHN FINNEMORE

A POTTER.

PEEPS AT
MANY LANDS

HOME LIFE IN INDIA

AN INDIAN GIRL.

PEEPS AT MANY LANDS

HOME LIFE IN INDIA

BY

JOHN FINNEMORE

CONTAINING TWELVE FULL-PAGE ILLUSTRATIONS
BY
MORTIMER MENPES

A. & C. BLACK, LTD.,
4, 5 & 6 SOHO SQUARE, LONDON, W.
1917

CONTENTS

CHAPTER		PAGE
I.	THE HOME OF THE RYOT	1
II.	AMONG THE VILLAGE FOLK—I.	5
III.	AMONG THE VILLAGE FOLK—II.	12
IV.	AMONG THE VILLAGE FOLK—III.	19
V.	AMONG THE VILLAGE FOLK—IV.	26
VI.	THE SPORTS OF THE VILLAGE	35
VII.	HOW THE VILLAGE IS RULED	42
VIII.	OFF TO THE MELA	47
IX.	INDIAN JUGGLERS	53
X.	HOMES IN THE CITY	60
XI.	FROM BIRTH TO MARRIAGE	67
XII.	THE HOME OF THE RAJAH	73
XIII.	HOMES OF THE WILD FOLK	81

LIST OF ILLUSTRATIONS

1.	AN INDIAN GIRL	*Frontispiece*
		FACING PAGE
2.	A WOMAN AT THE WELL	9
3.	A POTTER	16
4.	THE VILLAGE POET	25
5.	EVENING IN THE VILLAGE	32
6.	BY THE SACRED RIVER	41
7.	NATIVE SHOPS	48
8.	A BEGGAR	57
9.	A BULLOCK-CART	64
10.	A MINSTRELS' BALCONY	73
11.	THE RAJAH'S ELEPHANT	80
12.	AN INDIAN BOY	*On the Cover*

PREFATORY NOTE

THE first world of which a child has knowledge is, of course, the little world of home. As his interests extend, it is but natural that he should feel a curiosity as to the homes of children of other lands. He may be quite content with his own nest; he may sing, with Mr. Stevenson,

> "Little Indian, Sioux, or Crow,
> Little frosty Eskimo,
> Little Turk or Japanee,
> Oh, don't you wish that you were me?"

and, at the same time, take the keenest pleasure in hearing of the everyday round amid surroundings so different from his own. This series will give clear and vivid pictures of homes under other skies, and thus form an introduction to the life of the world under the conditions of existence which the child-imagination can grasp most easily.

INDIA

I

THE HOME OF THE RYOT

"Tell me, Hindu, tell me truly, in your home is nothing more
Than some tatties, and some chatties, and some pratties on the floor?
Quoth the Hindu, 'Nothing more.'"

Now, a tattie is a screen woven of grass, and a chatty is a water-vessel, so that with these and some kind of bedstead or bedding the furnishing of a Hindu home would seem to be a very simple affair. The above lines are, of course, written in a humorous vein, but for all that they contain a great deal of truth. There is scarcely a simpler home in the world than that of the Indian ryot, the husbandman, one of those many millions of quiet, simple, brown-faced men whose patient, never-ending labour lies at the base of all the wealth of India.

Let us glance at an Indian peasant village, lying in the vast plain of the Punjaub, and basking in the hot sun which follows the winter rains. The vast stretch of level land spreads like a sea from horizon to horizon, and, like the sea in some lights, it is green, for it is one huge carpet of young wheat. Nothing breaks the smooth run of the country save the village, which rises like an ant-heap in a flat meadow. It is no tiny hill upon which it stands, but it is raised upon the ruins of many former villages, and when this hamlet crumbles to the ground, fresh huts will stand upon a pedestal a foot higher than to-day.

Around the village lie a number of shallow tanks, dug in the soil, and filled with pools of water after the rains. These tanks are the cradle of the hamlet. From them the mud was dug to build the houses, and so they were formed. From them the mud will be taken afresh when new houses are wanted, and so they will grow larger. Mud is all the peasant needs to build his simple abode. Mud are the walls, mud the floors, and very often roofs also are of mud, though some builders use thatch. There are no windows, no chimneys. The latter are not often needed, for cooking is generally carried on out of doors. But when the rains drive the housewife within to boil the rice or bake the wheaten cakes at the fireplace, built of a few mud bricks, the smoke eddies about the room until it finds its way out at the door.

When you enter one of these single-roomed mud cottages, you are surprised to see how little it contains, and with what slight means the ryot can carry on his existence. You are not certain to discover even a bedstead, for in some huts there is none, but each inmate curls himself up in a blanket and lies contentedly on the floor. There are no chairs or tables, for the people sit on the floor and eat from it; and when the housewife cleans the latter, she plasters it with cow-dung. You look in vain for a hundred things which you would call necessities in a home. But the ryot does not need them, and does not feel the want of them. If he has a shelter from the rain, his plot of land to grow food for himself and his family, a blanket to wrap himself against the cold, one or two strips of cotton cloth for clothing, he is quite satisfied. We read of the man who took up his bed and walked ; the ryot very often could take up his bed and all the furniture of his house and run with it, so easy would be the load.

Yet we must not think that he is bound to be poor. As a rule he is poor—very poor—a man whose income is a penny or twopence a day, and his whole belongings scarce worth a sovereign. But his simple style of living is not always a sign of poverty. In a mud hut you may see a woman and her daughters busy about the household work with great silver bangles clustering on their wrists. Those form the family wealth. Into them the spare cash has been put ; and if the ryot has more rupees still, he stows them away in a secret hole in the ground. He does this because he knows nothing of banks, and would not trust them if he did. But he has heard of thieves, and takes great care that no one shall know where he has hidden his pile of silver coins. It will happen at times that, by some accident, he dies without having told anyone where to find the family treasure, and then there is great weeping and wailing, and his heirs are very sorrowful.

The ryot's week has seven working days, and his holidays are very few and far between ; and the implements with which he tills his field are as simple as his furniture. He has a plough which is a mere piece of bent wood, scratching the soil as the harnessed bull or buffalo drags it along. He has a rude spade, and a heavy mattock, and a fork, and with these he prepares the soil and grows his crops.

He works from daybreak to sunset. He is off to the field at dawn, taking some food with him to support him till noon, when his wife brings his dinner. He eats it, lies down for a sleep in the nearest shade, gets to work again about three, and labours till sunset. His wife does the work of the household and her share in the toil of the fields. Her household labours largely depend on the nearness of water and fuel. Sometimes she has to go a great distance to a well, a tank, or a stream, to draw her water, sometimes a long way to a patch of jungle to cut wood. In many parts wood is very scarce, and then she collects cow-dung and works it up into "cakes," and dries the latter in the sun for fuel.

The ryot's wife displays wonderful industry and thriftiness. She may be seen carefully sweeping a field of corn or rice after harvest with a hand-broom to draw together any grains that may have fallen. She watches the crops closely as they ripen, and carefully gathers the forward ears, lest they should shed their contents before the rest are ready. And when she grinds the corn for the family meal, she judges to a marvel how much grain to take, so that not a pinch shall be wasted. It is not often that she sets rice before her household, for, except in districts where rice grows in great plenty, it is far too great a luxury for the ryot's fare. As a rule, he eats the coarser kinds of grain, such as millet and pulse, and spices his food with salt, or sharp, pungent herbs and chillies.

II

AMONG THE VILLAGE FOLK—I

In many a large village of India, life goes on just as it went on five hundred years ago. The people of the village know that the white masters rule the land; they pay taxes, perhaps, to the British Raj—the British Government—but they very rarely see a white face, and they live their own life under their own native headmen, as they have always done. Very often the native huts are clustered together in a village, which may have from a hundred to a thousand houses in it. This custom comes down from times when bands of marauders swept across the land, and no man felt safe unless his home lay within the shelter of the mud or stone wall which encircled the local hamlet. These walls still exist in many places, though the British peace now lies over India, and within them is to be found the ancient, old-world village life of the Indian farmer, artisan, and peasant.

The streets of the village are very narrow—mere alleys threading their way among the rows of mud huts in which the peasants live. These close-packed houses suffer very severely when fire breaks out. The flame leaps from thatch to thatch, from street to street, and the fires are most furious in the scorching heat of summer, when everything that will burn is like tinder. Very often a whole village will be destroyed, and the homeless people are left without shelter or food, for their store of grain has been burned with the rest of their belongings. They beg help, or borrow money, wherever they can, and rebuild their ruined homes.

The home of a well-to-do farmer stands in the village, though his farm may be two or three miles away. It is entered through a main gate in a high mud wall, and the wall will run right round his premises, so that all, men and beasts, must pass in or out at the one point. Inside the gate is an open hall, where male visitors are received and the men of the family sit when they are at leisure. Next comes an open space, beyond which lies the house proper, a mud and thatch building, containing a large room, where the members of the family eat and sleep, a store-house, and a kitchen. The dining and bedroom is as bare as the house of the ryot, and the family bedding consists of a few mats and pillows rolled up and set in a corner. The store-house is filled with grain, and the kitchen is stocked with vessels of brass and earthenware, for cooking, eating, and carrying water. The cattle-sheds are built at the eastern side of the house ; at other points granaries are set up ; and the rest of the enclosure is a garden where herbs and plants are grown for the kitchen.

The work of this house, and of every other house in the village, begins very early in the morning. The first glimpse of the morning star is the signal for everyone to rise. The peasants set off to the fields, and the farmer urges his labourers with the cry : "Haste, haste, the star has risen !" From the mud temple of the village comes the loud blast of a holy shell blown by a priest: he is awaking the village gods. Travellers rise and resume their journey. Schoolboys are seen running to school, and the work of the day begins in earnest.

Numbers of the men go down to the river or to the village tank to bathe, while the women sprinkle the front and back yards of their dwellings with cow-dung. This is done to drive away the goddess of ill-luck, who will not come to a place where the cow, a sacred animal in the eyes of all Hindus, is present. Next the women sweep out their houses, milk the cows and goats, clean their cooking-vessels, and make ready the first meal. To this the men return at about eight o'clock, and sit down on the ground to eat rice or *chuppaties*. The latter are flat, round, unleavened cakes of meal, and form the daily bread of both rich and poor. With these foods they use various sauces and condiments, pickles and curries, and drink buttermilk. When the men have finished eating, the women take what is left in the dishes. The food is eaten from brass plates or plantain-leaves, and raised to the mouth with the hands.

The men now go back to their labour in the fields or their workshops, and the women fetch water, collect fuel, weave, pound rice or grain, grind spices for curry powder, and get the midday meal ready and serve it at noon. This is mainly of rice and vegetables, served with curds and the usual sauces; and after dinner comes a break while they rest and await the heat of noon to pass. The supper-hour is eight o'clock, when the remainder of the food prepared that day is eaten. But among some classes fresh food is made ready for every meal, for it is a law with them to throw or give away all food left uneaten at a meal. Soon after supper all retire to bed, for they must be afoot at early dawn.

The busiest spot in the village is the well, for women are coming and going to it all day long. They stand and chatter and laugh while each in turn fills her tall water-jar, and then, when the jar is filled and balanced on her head, moves away with swift, graceful carriage. Some have good whole robes, some are in little better than rags, but everyone has a corner of her robe drawn across her face as a veil, and the veil is never dropped until she is within her own door. A little beyond the well, and seated full in the sun, is a very strange figure. It is that of an old man, almost naked, and very thin, every bone starting through the skin of his meagre body, and his legs and arms looking like mere sticks. From head to foot he is plastered with mud and filth, and his wild eyes glitter through a tangle of matted hair. He takes no notice of anyone, but stares straight before him as if lost in thought; and when the women see him, they become silent. It is a beggar—a religious mendicant.

Now there comes round a corner near at hand a Hindu gentleman, very handsomely dressed. He wears a great turban of pink muslin and a rich robe of silk; he shines in the sun like a flower. He walks forward without seeing the beggar, and all of a sudden the latter bursts into an angry roar, and assails the gentleman with a torrent of abuse. He calls him every name you could imagine, and a great many you could not imagine, and the politest of them all is to call him the son of a dog and a pig, two very unclean animals. What is wrong? Why, the gentleman

A WOMAN AT THE WELL.

came so near the beggar that his shadow fell on the latter. And what reply does he make to the stream of angry language? He bows most respectfully, and entreats pardon in the most abject tones, for at a glance he has read the painted marks on the beggar's face.

This seems all very strange, but it is really quite simple: the beggar is a high-caste Hindu, the rich man is of a lower caste, and his shadow, to the beggar, is unclean. What is caste? Caste is the class into which every Hindu is born. There are four great castes: the priest caste, the warrior caste, the merchant caste, and the labourer caste. But these castes have been so divided and subdivided that there are now thousands of castes in India, and every member of each caste looks upon the other members as brothers, and those outside his own caste as strangers and men apart from him. In whatever caste a Hindu is born, to that he belongs to the day of his death, unless he is deprived of it. He may fall out of caste, but he can never rise to a higher one. He loses caste by breaking the laws of caste. It would be impossible to say here what all those laws are, for they are very numerous, but these are a few of the chief. Men may only marry in their own caste, eat with their own caste, or touch food prepared either by a man of their own caste or a man of higher caste. No man may allow another of lower caste to touch his cooked food, or even to enter the room where it is being made ready. The higher-caste man is defiled if a lower caste touches him, or brushes against him, or if he allows the shadow of an inferior to fall upon him. A Hindu may not marry a widow or leave India without losing caste. He at once loses caste if he becomes a Christian or a Moslem.

What is the punishment of a man who loses caste? It is the most thoroughgoing boycott in the world. His friends and relatives and all the members of his caste give him the cold shoulder at once. They will not speak with him, eat with him, drink with him, smoke with him. His children remain unmarried, and this is a terrible thing in Hindu eyes, for no family will be connected with him in any form. He cannot obtain the services of a priest, a barber, or a washerman, and he is refused aid at every turn of his way. The caste system is of tremendous power in Hindu social life, and its whole might is directed with crushing force against the man who has broken his caste and been driven out from his fellows.

The consequence is that the Hindu will do anything sooner than break a law of caste. He will starve rather than touch food which may have been defiled in any way by an inferior; if he is a bad man, he will cheerfully commit every crime in the criminal calendar, but he will not offend against caste. And, finally, caste is the one subject upon which every Hindu will tell the truth. No man can have dealings with a stranger unless he is sure of the latter's caste, and the stranger will be bound to tell truly to what order he belongs. Caste is the be-all and end-all of the Hindu. He may be false to everything else, but never to that.

Caste is not a matter of wealth or position. The highest caste includes beggars who scarce know where to find a handful of rice; the lowest may have men of great wealth among its members. So now we see why the beggar roared out in angry and haughty disdain, and why the finely dressed merchant bent low and asked pardon humbly, and made haste to get out of the way. The one is a Brahmin, a member of the priestly caste, and the other a man of lower caste. And if that rich merchant were to bribe with all his wealth—ay, and a hundred times his wealth—he could not persuade the poorest Hindu to look upon him as the equal of the naked beggar.

III

AMONG THE VILLAGE FOLK—II

THE group near the well breaks up. The merchant hurries from the spot, the women run off with their water, and the Brahmin mendicant also goes his way, still muttering angrily, for he must now busy himself with his purification. He must wash the caste mark from his forehead, perform many ablutions, and again smear himself with earth, ashes, and cow-dung before he can be clean from the defilement of the merchant's shadow.

A little farther is a large shed under a great tree, and round the shed are broken carts, and planks of wood lie about. This is the carpenter's shop, and the carpenter is a very important man in the village, for he is one of the five useful artisans of Indian life. The others are the potter, the shoemaker, the weaver, and the blacksmith. With these men ready to work in wood, in pottery, in leather, in weaving, in iron, the village can exist without outside help : it is sufficient in itself at every point.

Here, again, caste comes in. Each trade forms a caste of its own, and all born within the trade follow it. There is no talk in a Hindu family of what a boy shall be, or what he would like to be. That is settled from the moment of his birth. If he be born in a carpenter's family, he will be a carpenter ; in a weaver's family, he will be a weaver; the son of a potter will become a potter; and so on. In this way there is a great inherited skill in the fingers of an Indian workman when he comes to practise his craft, and the carpenter whose shed we are approaching can afford us a striking proof of this. Among his tools there is one of which he makes great use, a peculiar kind of adze. This tool is very difficult to manage in the hands of an unskilled workman, yet there, just within the shed, is the carpenter's son, a little thin boy, barely ten years old, using it with the greatest dexterity. A grown man, not of the carpenter caste, could not use it so well after five years' practice. But that boy's ancestors for a hundred generations have been swinging that tool, and their skill lives again in him.

The carpenter is hard at work on a new cart, and he is clad only in a turban and a waistcloth, and we notice that he has a thread across his shoulders. This is the sacred thread which shows that he belongs to one of the five orders of great artisans. He has always plenty of work to do, for he must make yokes, ploughs, and handles for tools, door-posts, doors, rafters, bedsteads, and wooden spoons. He builds the carts which are drawn by the slow-moving bullocks, and at times he has to build a great car on which the village idol is borne in state at the annual festival. If he is a clever carver, he is sometimes employed to carve the image of a village god, and when it is set up in the temple he receives a handsome present.

Each farmer for whom he works gives him so much grain, and he charges a certain amount for making special things, such as finely carved bedsteads for well-to-do people, and ornamental door-posts and decorations for fine houses. But, as a rule, he is not paid a great deal in money; people give him food and things which he needs, in return for his labour, and so he makes a comfortable living.

As this is a large village, there is bound to be a blacksmith in it, for the farmers and peasants need the carpenter and the blacksmith above all other craftsmen. His shop is proclaimed, as it is in every country, by the clang of hammers, and by the knot of men standing about, waiting for their tools to be mended or new ones to be made. His tools are very simple. He has a few hammers, some pincers, and a pair of bellows. Yet he does all the iron work of the village, and gives satisfaction to his customers. He makes hinges, locks, and keys for doors; spades, reaping hooks, axes, sickles, and crowbars for work in the woods and fields; knives and choppers for use in the kitchen; and many other implements.

The tap-tap of lighter hammers calls us to the workshop of the goldsmith, who lives a little farther on. Every large village has its goldsmith, and he is one of the busiest workers in the place. Not only are the Indian peasants very fond of jewellery, but, as we have seen, the spare cash of the household is turned into ornaments and worn by the women. From morning till night women are coming and going to the shop of the goldsmith. One brings a small bag of coins to be made into a bangle, a necklet, a nose-ring, an ear-ring, or an anklet; another has a broken ornament which needs mending; a third has an old ornament which she wishes him to melt down and remake in a new shape.

But the goldsmith is a sad rogue. Of all the craftsmen in the village, he has by far the worst character. He is full of cunning, and the sly tricks by which he cheats the simple country folk are legion. A woman brings a piece of gold to be made into a rich bangle. It is made. Some time afterwards the family needs money, and the ornament is turned into cash. But the purchaser only offers half of the value of the original gold. Why ? The goldsmith has filled the inside of the bangle with copper and kept part of the gold for himself. The country people tell stories without end of the thievish tricks and sly ways of the goldsmith, and here is one of them.

One day a woman brought a bag of rupees to a goldsmith, and told him to make them into a silver bangle, and he promised he would do so at once. But his promise was, as usual, worth nothing at all, and the woman came time after time, and the bangle was not ready. At last she flew into a great rage, called him by every kind of evil name, and said that she would not leave his workshop without either the bangle or the rupees. The goldsmith seemed to pay no heed to a word that she said, and went on shaping a nose-ring as if she had not been there. The truth was that he had nothing to say: he had spent every one of the rupees, and knew not what to do. The woman spread her upper garments on the floor, lay down on them, and said once more that there she would stay, day and night, till she had her own. The day was very hot, the woman had walked a long way, and was very tired, and before long she fell asleep. Now the cunning goldsmith saw his chance. He slipped to her side and rubbed a certain kind of gum on her eyelids. Then he went back to his work and made such a noise with his hammer that the woman woke up. When she found she could not open her eyes, she cried out in terror, and called upon the goldsmith for help.

"Is there something wrong ?" asked the goldsmith in tones of wonder.

"I am blind !" cried the woman. "I cannot open my eyes. Oh, what shall I do ? What has happened to me ?"

"Ah !" said the goldsmith, "I see what has happened. You came here and called me by every evil name you could think of. I bore your abuse in silence and patience. But the goddess of our craft will not be so patient ; she has struck you blind for reviling me."

"What can I do to regain my sight ?" said the woman. "I have many children and a husband to care for."

"There's only one thing to be done," replied the goldsmith, gravely. "You must make an offering to my goddess, and then she will forgive."

"Gladly will I do it," cried the poor woman. "Take every rupee that I brought to you and offer them up to her, if that will give me back my sight."

"It is enough," said the goldsmith ; and he took some cold water and washed the woman's eyes, and she found, to her great joy, that she could see as well as ever. Then she went away, thanking the goldsmith for restoring her sight, and marvelling at the wonderful power of the goddess of the goldsmith's craft.

As we leave the goldsmith's house, we meet the *dhoby*, the village washerman, and his wife, carrying along the

A POTTER

street the big bundles of dirty clothes they have just collected from the houses of the village. They go to the houses together, because the *dhoby* himself may not venture into the women's apartments, so his wife goes there to fetch the soiled clothes of the women, and often stays a long time to tell the ladies what is going on in the village. The wife of the *dhoby* carries the dirty garments on a hooked stick, for she would be defiled by their touch; but the *dhoby* himself is free from that caste rule, and his shoulders are loaded with as big a burden as he can carry. Behind them comes one of their children, carrying a big pot. In this is placed the food which the washerwoman has collected from the customers as part payment for her husband and herself.

The *dhoby* is used for all kinds of odd jobs as well as washing, and thus he has won the name of "son of the village," and his wife is the "daughter of the village." The village people supply him and his wife with a hut on some patch of ground belonging to the village, give them food and a little money, and some small presents when the *dhoby* makes himself useful at a wedding or a funeral. If it is a long way to the river or tank where he washes the clothes, they supply him with a donkey or two to carry the packs; but if the water is near at hand, he and his family must carry the bundles for themselves. At the waterside the clothes are dipped and rinsed and beaten against stones till the dirt is driven out of them, starched, and laid out to bleach and dry in the sun. Next they are folded and packed ready to take back to their owners. The *dhoby* and his wife may have to wash hundreds of garments, large and small, at a time, and the owners never mark their clothes, yet the *dhoby* never makes a mistake. He has his own marks, and they serve him well ; the pile of clothes handed in at each door is certain to be correct.

As a rule, the *dhoby* and his wife are very poor, and are dressed in rags. But on great occasions they will come out as grand as anyone. This is because they claim the right to use the clothes which may be in their hands at any time. At a wedding the *dhoby* attends in a rich robe belonging to a village magnate ; the *dhoby's* wife is draped in a beautiful *sari*, a gown which is the property of the wife of the wealthy money-lender. The owners turn a blind eye on these birds who thus flaunt in their fine feathers ; it is an understood thing, and if the clothes are brought home in a day or so, nicely washed and neatly folded, no notice is taken.

IV

AMONG THE VILLAGE FOLK—III

THE noontide heat is now past, and the boys are going back to school. They take their way to a large mud and thatch building in the shade of a great tree, and enter the door. This is the school, and it is built and kept in repair by the village. It is an old-fashioned native school, and inside there are no desks or seats, no books as we know them, or slates or paper. Pens there are, but no ink. The floor is strewn with sand, and the boys sit down upon it. At one end of the room is a bank of sand, and here the teacher sits upon a reed mat.

As each boy enters, he goes to his bookcase, takes his book, and sits down to learn his lesson. The bookcase is formed of two pieces of wood bound together by a cord. Inside are a number of palm leaves with writing on their faces. These are the boys' books, and every boy has his own case, so that perhaps forty or fifty cases are hanging on the wall of the school. When the time for the writing lesson comes, the boys use pens made of a sharpened stick of wood, or a reed, and form the characters in a smoothed-out bed of sand. Some of the advanced scholars write on palm-leaves with a reed pen.

The boys go to school at break of day, and are there

for two or three hours before breakfast. Each must take care that he has marked his forehead with the sacred ash, in honour of the god Siva, or he will be severely punished by his teacher. From eight to nine he has his breakfast. School goes on again from nine to twelve, when he goes home to his dinner. The afternoon session runs from about two to six, when the school closes for the day.

Sometimes the schoolmaster is the village poet, sometimes he is a Hindu scholar ; quite often he is a rather ignorant man, who has hit upon that way of making a living. If he knows his own language and a little arithmetic, he will give perfect satisfaction to the parents of his scholars. He does not know, and they do not know, anything of the world outside India, and little enough of their own country outside their own province, but that does not trouble them. In geography the master divides the oceans into milk oceans and fire oceans, the rivers into *ghee* (butter) rivers and honey rivers. He has heard of the mighty Himalaya Mountains, and tells his pupils that the world rests on them. But many of these teachers are really good at simple arithmetic, and handle numbers with ease and freedom. They teach reading and writing, arithmetic as far as fractions, the composing of letters and essays, and store their pupils' minds with a wealth of proverbs and wise sayings. Where the master is a Hindu scholar, the upper classes study grammar and the great Indian classics, the *Mahabharata* and the *Ramayana*.

The master expects a small payment in money from the parents of each scholar, more or less, as the parents are rich or poor, and offerings of food, especially at harvest-time, when measures of grain are sent to him. If the teacher finds he has not enough to live upon, he will send his scholars to sing through the streets of the village, at which time they beg for him at every house, and carry to him the offerings. Once a year comes the school festival, when worship is offered to the goddess Sarasvati, the Goddess of Knowledge. The boys are dressed in their brightest and freshest robes, and the master and his scholars go from house to house, singing and performing and collecting money for the celebration. In a large village, or if the scholars come from smaller hamlets in the neighbourhood, a whole week or more will be spent in this way, and it is the most joyous time of the school-boys' year. When the collection is ended, the master takes the greater part of it for himself, and the rest is spent in giving the boys a treat.

Holidays are not frequent. When the moon is new, and when it is full, the school is closed for two days, making four days in the month. The school is also closed on the day of a great Hindu festival, and for a few days at the beginning of the year. There are no long holidays in a native school. As for the boys' life in school, a native writer says: "The method of teaching in the village academy is very peculiar. The boys are asked to bring their lessons one by one. Some boys are allowed to write in the sand on the floor, some on the palm-leaves; some are studying their lessons; some are repeating their lessons to the teacher; some are undergoing punishment for not studying their lessons properly. The punishments of the boys are exceedingly severe. A boy under punishment is placed in a corner of the school, and required to stand on one leg while the other is bent and held in his hand. Here a boy is left a long time in a bending attitude; there another is made to sit and stand a hundred or even two hundred times in succession without ceasing. Another boy is hung up by his hands. While the boy is hanging, a sharp knife is fixed on the ground, projecting upwards so that he may not rest his feet on the ground. Sometimes the student is kept in a bending attitude, and another boy is made to ride on his back. And at times the student has to starve the whole day; and not infrequently the teacher unmercifully wields his cane of office."

Now we see how things go on in a boys' school; and as for a girls' school, it would be useless to look for such a thing. The girls of the village are at home, helping their mothers, and they are never taught anything but domestic duties.

Still farther on, at the edge of the village, stands the shed of the potter, whose trade is one of the oldest and most famous crafts in the land. He sits at his wheel, surrounded by shreds and fragments of pots which have failed, and turns out with steady, skilful hand the host of pots which the village requires. Trade is never slack with him. In the house of the poorest ryot there are ten or a dozen pots; in the house of the wealthy farmer there are three or four hundred. And besides the breakages of every day, when a birth or death happens in the family, every pot becomes unclean, and is broken in pieces, and replaced with new vessels from the potter.

Among the Village Folk

It is most interesting to watch the potter at his work. He has a simple wheel, which in shape has not been altered for thousands of years. A hundred generations ago his father's fathers used the potters' wheel and shaped the vessels with the thumb or a small piece of wood, and so does he to-day. Upon the wheel he places a mass of wet clay, and the wheel begins to spin. Under the deft touches of his thumb the clay begins swiftly to take the shape he has in mind : a long neck draws out above, a globe-like body opens out below, and soon there is a pot, one of a certain number of shapes, each useful for a certain purpose. The potter has a fixed round of designs. The idea of asking for a new kind of pot would never enter the head of any housewife, and if it did she would not get it. Custom is sacred : his father always made pots in certain sizes and shapes ; the potter will do the same, and so will his son after him.

When the vessels are made, they are set in the sun to dry and burned in a kiln, the fire in which is often fed with the refuse of the village. Yet the pot is clean, and even a Brahmin may drink from it, for, as the old rhyme runs :

> "Though the clay be base and the potter mean,
> The pot brings water to make souls clean."

Still, though the high-class Hindu may drink from the pot, he must break it afterwards ; such is the law of his caste. The low caste may keep the pot unbroken and use it again.

The potter makes earthen vessels for many purposes :

for cooking food; for carrying water from the well; for storing grain and provisions; for keeping valuables; for carrying food to the fields—in short, at almost every turn of a native's life there is some use for one or another of the many vessels purchased from the potter. Besides articles of use, he shapes images in clay, images of gods and goddesses, of men, women, and children, of beasts and birds, rudely formed and painted, to be used as idols for shrines or offerings to a temple.

As we return along the main street, we see a man standing near the well, a wretched-looking man in a ragged turban, and plastered with mud, as if he had just finished a very dirty piece of work. He is uttering from time to time a mournful cry, but no one seems to attend to him. Is he a beggar? No; he is the village *toty*, the scavenger and sweeper, the man who does the dirtiest work about the place, the menial of the hamlet. What does he want? The poor fellow is very thirsty, and would like a drink of cool water from the well. Why does he not draw it at once. Ah! he dare not do that on any account. He is a man of no caste at all, an outcaste—a Pariah—a man to whom the most defiling tasks can be given. If he were to touch the well or the water, both would become unclean, and the villagers, even of the lowest caste, would not drink from the polluted source. Nor will anyone among them allow the *toty* to enter his house, for the place would become defiled by his mere presence.

Again the *toty* raises his sad cry, and now a kind-hearted woman comes from a house near at hand and brings a pitcher to the well. She fills it and approaches the

THE VILLAGE POET.

sweeper. But she takes care not to touch him, nor does she allow him to touch her vessel. If she did, she would have to break the pitcher at once. But the *toty* stands at a safe distance, and deftly knits his hands into a cup. The woman pours water into the hollow of his hands, and he drinks and is refreshed.

V

AMONG THE VILLAGE FOLK—IV

A cloud of dust now rises at the far end of the village street. It moves forward, and we can see a flock of sheep coming on, passing through the village on their way from pasture to pasture. They are in charge of two or three men, quiet, simple-looking fellows, who stare round them in wonder, gazing upon the houses and alleys of the village as a countryman gazes on the sights of a great town. And the village is a wonder to them, for these are shepherds—men who spend their lives in lonely places where no two huts stand together, men whose days are passed in the open field, and to whom a roof over their heads would be a strange and new thing. Each man carries a heavy iron-shod staff, which serves him for support and as a weapon against the wild beasts which love to prey on his flock. His sheep have many enemies. He must be ever on the watch against wolves, jackals, and foxes, and sometimes the fierce and terrible tiger swoops down on his helpless charges. But the shepherd never deserts his sheep. He is famous for the care and kindness which he shows to his flock. If he loses a sheep or a lamb in the thickest jungle, he will search day and night until it is found, when he bears it back on his shoulders with great joy.

Among the Village Folk

A shepherd is called an *eddaiar*, from the word *eddai*, which means "middle." This is because they used to live in the middle grounds, the land between the naked mountains and the cultivated farms—places where they could find grazing for their flocks without fear of trespassing on the crops. As they live apart from other men, and have no share in the village life which sharpens wits, they are very simple and ignorant. The villagers love to tell stories of shepherds—stories which show the childlike simplicity of these wanderers in lonely places. Here is one of the stories :

One day a money-lender was going to a distant village with a large bag of rupees to lend to the ryots at great interest. He took a shepherd with him to guide him and protect him on the road, and the shepherd carried five pieces of money in a bag at his waist—all the money he possessed. But night fell before they reached the village, and they lost their way in thick jungle. Nothing could be done before morning, so the money-lender told the shepherd to lie down and rest, and be sure neither to move nor make a sound, while he would hide himself and his bag of rupees in some thick bushes near at hand. At midnight a band of robbers passed that way, and one of them stumbled over the shepherd.

"Here's a log in the way," said the robber.

"A log !" cried the simple shepherd ; "and do you suppose a log could have five pieces of money in a bag at its waist ?"

"It is a man," said the chief of the robbers ; "seize him and search him !"

This was done, and the shepherd lost his money. As the robbers went away, one of them said: " This money feels rather light. Perhaps it is bad."

The shepherd was angry when he heard the robber cast doubts on his money, and shouted out: " But, indeed, it is nothing of the sort. And if you don't believe me, just ask the money-lender who is over there in the bushes."

" A money-lender !" cried the robbers in delight, and ran to seize him. They searched the bushes, and had him in their grip in a twinkling. They not only took his bag of rupees, but gave him a tremendous beating into the bargain, for everyone hates a money-lender. And the next morning the money-lender had to creep home without his money, but with a body full of sore bones, and vowing that he would never again engage a simple shepherd to journey with him.

So the day wears on in the village, and as the dusk draws near, the mothers call in the children playing in the village street. The word has gone round that wolves have been seen near the hamlet, and the dusk is a favourite time for one of these savage creatures to dash down the village street, seize one of the playing children in its jaws, and carry it off into the jungle. Great numbers of children in certain parts of India are carried off and devoured by wolves. Sometimes one charges into the village, sometimes there are two. In the latter case one wolf calls off the attention of the people, while the second seizes a baby and escapes with it.

It is on record that one wolf carried away more than seventy children; it was the terror of a whole country-side, and was well known because of its peculiar way of running. At length it was shot by an English officer, with a baby in its jaws. He found that the dreaded creature was a small she-wolf, an under-sized, mangy little beast, with a lame leg. Very likely its lameness was the reason why it took to seizing children : it was not swift enough to catch its usual prey.

The Indian natives believe firmly that children are sometimes spared, and, instead of being eaten, are suckled by the mother-wolf and brought up with the wolf cubs. Many cases have been known of these wolf children. They have been found living with wolves in a den, running on all fours, tearing the food with their teeth, and biting severely those who captured them. One boy was found when he was about seven years old, and he was a wolf in all his actions and ways. He ran about on his elbows and knees ; he ripped off clothes when they were put on him ; he ate from the ground, and tore meat from a bone with his teeth. In time he was taught to walk on his feet and wear clothing, but he could never be taught to use human speech, though he would gnash his teeth and growl and snarl like a wolf. The only human habit he developed was that of smoking cigars, and if one were given him he would puff at it with signs of the most hearty enjoyment.

But we must now go back to our village.

Here comes a herd of buffaloes returning from the swamp a mile away. What huge, shaggy, fierce-looking creatures they are, with their wild eyes, tossing manes, and great, spreading, sharp-pointed horns! Yet the watcher of the buffaloes is not a man, nor even a youth ;

he is a tiny, dark-skinned, naked little boy, barely seven years old. But he sits on the leading buffalo as proudly as a king on his throne, and screams orders in his small shrill voice, and thwacks his huge charges with a stick, and is obeyed as promptly as possible. Upon gaining the village street the herd breaks up, and every buffalo seeks the shed of its master. To-morrow morning they will reassemble, and the child will take them to the swamp again to feed.

It is his father's buffalo on which the boy is riding, and as he reaches his own door, his mother comes out to welcome him. The child at once begins to relate the happenings of the day. There was a big tiger in the swamp; the boy saw him two or three times, and saw his footmarks many times, as the great savage beast circled about the herd, hoping to cut off a straggler and kill it, and drag it off for food. The mother listens with interest, but without fear for the child's safety. The tiger might be the biggest and fiercest of his kind, but the boy, amid his buffaloes, was as safe as in his own home. On such an occasion as this the intelligence of the big shaggy beasts is wonderful. No sooner do they scent a tiger than they draw together and face him, with the tiny herdsman in their midst. The tiger will never charge them. He knows better. Those long sharp horns, those stamping hoofs, would soon make short work of him. A single buffalo will make a splendid stand against a tiger, and a number would kill him easily. The tiger's chance is to catch one unawares, and spring upon it, and deal a fatal blow before it can face round and get its terrible horns to work.

Next come the cows and goats from the pastures near at hand, and the women are soon busy milking and fastening them up in the sheds for the night. The men arrive at all times, some early and some late, for the latter have perhaps walked three or four miles home from distant fields. After supper comes the leisure hour of the day. The villagers meet to chat, and smoke, and chew betel-nuts, and a favourite place is near the well in the shade of a great tamarind-tree.

Here the gossip of the village passes, and the crops and the weather are discussed as countrymen discuss them everywhere. Perhaps among the company may be the village poet, or a wandering poet who passes from hamlet to hamlet, singing songs and begging. As a rule, the poet is a very poor man, and earns a great portion of his living by writing a poem in praise of a wealthy neighbour, who is then expected to make him a present. When the villagers are at leisure he amuses them with songs and stories, or, if they are in a serious mood, he recites and explains to them portions of the great Indian classics, such as the *Mahabharata*. The villagers sit down to listen to him after supper, and often half the night will pass while he recites and expounds portions of a great poem, and his audience listens with the greatest attention.

At seasons of the year when work does not press, this nightly session may be continued for several months, and at the end of the period each listener pays a small sum to the poet, or gives him a present of food or grain, or new clothes or an ornament.

The poet has a wonderful memory, which is stored with

songs, stories, poems, anecdotes, and proverbs, so that he can meet every occasion of life with some fitting verses or tale, and can suit every audience with a poem or a story adapted to their understanding. On this evening the village poet is with the company under the tamarind-tree, and he is amusing them with this story:

Once upon a time there was a jackal, who lived in a hole under a rock at the foot of a great mountain, where many great and powerful wild animals were to be found. Of all these animals the jackal was the poorest and meanest, and he had such great difficulty in finding food that his bones stood out through his hide. Yet, as we shall see, he found means to feed upon the grandest and most majestic of his neighbours. One day he saw a splendid elephant browsing on the shrubs of the valley, and he thought how fine it would be to feed upon the flesh of such a magnificent animal. So he ran to the elephant and bent low before him, and humbly begged him to listen for one moment.

"What have you to say?" asked the elephant.

"I wish to tell my lord the elephant," replied the jackal, "that I believe him to be the chief in all this country for beauty, and strength, and valour. Yet in the jungle at the foot of the valley there is an elephant who dares to speak in the most disrespectful manner of you and of your noble family."

"I will seek him out," said the elephant, "and teach him a lesson that he will not speedily forget." So he set off with slow and stately step towards the jungle.

But the jackal ran on ahead, slipping unseen through

EVENING IN THE VILLAGE.

the bushes, and made his way to the elephant of the jungle. To him he told a similar story, and when the two elephants met they engaged at once in a terrible battle, and in the end the first elephant was killed. The jackal had watched the fight from the jungle, and as soon as the winner went away he rushed to the place and began with great delight to feed upon the fallen elephant. He ate and ate until he had made his way into the elephant's stomach, where he still went on eating. Now, it was the hottest time of the year, and the elephant's body shrank in the great heat, and the opening into the stomach shrank also. Thus, when the jackal had eaten his fill, he could not get out, for the opening was smaller, and he had swollen himself with food. So he began to cry for help.

It happened that the great god Siva and his wife were passing that way, and they were very greatly astonished to hear a voice coming from the body of a dead elephant.

"There is some wonderful spirit shut up there," said Siva, and he approached the body, and called upon the spirit to reveal itself to him.

"I cannot," replied the voice, "unless you first send for the god Indra, the god of rain." In order to please the strange being, Siva sent for the god Indra, and with Indra came pouring rain and driving wind. Many other gods and goddesses came as well upon hearing of this remarkable being shut up in the body of a dead elephant. The rain soaked the dead body and swelled it, until the opening was as wide as it had been before. But when, instead of a wonderful spirit, only a mean jackal crept from the body of the elephant, then Siva and his friends laughed till they made the skies ring, and went to their own world greatly delighted with the joke.

The villagers, too, laugh with equal delight at the story of the cunning jackal, and then the meeting breaks up, and the men go home to bed. As they pass down the street they hear the cry of several jackals prowling round the village in search of food—a long, whining cry, which is answered by the yelps of the pariah dogs. These are miserable curs which belong to no man in particular, but slink about the village, mangy, half-starved and miserable, devouring every morsel of rubbish which is eatable, and so aiding the scavenger in his labours. Soon the last door is shut, the last dim light put out, and the pariah dogs have the village streets to themselves, and they scour hither and thither in search of garbage, and fight and snarl over any scrap of offal which falls in their way.

VI

THE SPORTS OF THE VILLAGE

IN their leisure hours the villagers amuse themselves in various ways; the older men play chess, the younger men and the boys play a kind of hockey, and a simple form of cricket. In the latter game one player holds both bat and ball and the rest field. The striker hits the ball into the air as high and as far as he can. The rest run to catch the ball, and the one who makes the catch takes the place of the striker. They also play at a game resembling "prisoner's base," and all, both old and young, are fond of flying kites.

In some parts where the villagers are active and athletic, they have bouts with the quarterstaff, and wrestle. In playing with the quarterstaff sometimes only the long stick is used; sometimes the player has both a stick and a shield, using the latter to intercept the blows of his opponent. In a well-matched contest with the quarterstaff a battle will often be fought out for a long time, and the play will be as clever and determined as ever was seen on a village green in the old days when our English yeomen were fond of this weapon. At times the players get so excited, and the combat so furious, that the older men have to interfere lest serious harm should be done.

But many of the village sports are not so innocent as these. The cruel sports of cock-fighting and ram-fighting are very favourite ones, and when a pair of famous birds or animals is matched, a great crowd of men will gather from many villages to watch the combat. A first-rate fighting cock is the pride of the village, and the wealthier inhabitants will wager heavy sums on him when he is entered to fight the bird which is the boast of a neighbouring hamlet. He is usually prepared for the battle by the village barber, who understands this work very well. As a native writer remarks:

"The village barbers are wonderful fellows for cock-fighting; they generally rear fighting cocks—often half a dozen of them. The barbers who delight in cock-fighting will carry their cocks even to a distance of ten miles, and there they will spend a whole day—without having any noontide meal—till nine or ten at night. If the cocks are wounded in fighting the men are full of anxiety concerning them. They chew a bit of dry ginger and blow into the mouth, nostrils, and ears of the wounded and fainting birds; they put a wet cloth on the head of the injured creature, and pour a few drops of water into its mouth in order to refresh it. If a barber happens to win with a bird, it is a day of great joy and victory for him. When he approaches his village, he sends for the parish drums, and, to the deafening noise of these drums, he marches through the dull streets of the village to his home. On the following day he runs down to the house of the goldsmith with a piece of silver, of which he wants a ring made to decorate the leg of his victorious bird."

Many Hindu and Moslem gentlemen, large landowners and rich merchants, have a great passion for ram-fighting, and great sums are spent in obtaining rams which have won a famous name in the ring, and still greater sums exchange hands according to the issue of the fight. The trainers of these rams teach the animals certain signs and words by which they can guide them in the combat, and the courage and resolution of these creatures is such that the cruel contest will continue for many hours. The owners of the rams lay such sums on their favourites that often they are ruined by the defeat of the animal, just as men ruin themselves in our own country by betting on race-horses.

When a big bull-fight is announced, the people throng from all the villages near at hand to the plain where the contest is to be held. This bull-fight is not in the least like the bull-fights held in some parts of Europe, or the bull-baiting which once took place in England. The bull, as a rule, is quite uninjured ; it is the men who have to look out for themselves. The owner of the bull turns him loose in an open space, and the bull has a new cloth tied round his neck. In this cloth there is a sum of money, and the man who can master the bull and take the cloth from his neck wins the cloth and the money.

When the spectators have taken their places, the crier beats a drum loudly, as a signal that the contest is about to begin. The master of the bull leads his animal to the centre of the open space, and there turns him loose, bidding him make the best of his way home to his shed. At the same moment a score of men place themselves in the bull's path, ready to do their utmost to win the prize. These men have no weapons in their hands ;

if they master the bull, it must be done by sheer strength and skill, so that it is a genuinely sporting affair. A well-trained bull understands perfectly well the rules of the game. He will stand quite still, keeping a most wary eye upon his opponents until a man springs at him and tries to secure a grip. Then the horns flash, or a leg delivers a kick, or he charges full on his enemy. Next he wheels like lightning, for a man has darted up on his flank, and now they come thick and fast against him from every side, and he strikes, kicks, charges, sending his opponents over like ninepins, and working his way through them until he is either caught and held or is clear of the ring. In the latter case he gallops off home. He is a victor, and he knows it. It can be seen in his joyous bounds and leaps.

Sometimes bulls are brought forward which very few men will care to face. They are old fighters, and such past masters of every trick in the game that they have never once been held. There is great danger, too, in tackling such a bull. He often wounds, and sometimes kills, his man, so that, however great a sum of money is in the cloth, no bull-fighter will venture against him. So the proud owner parades him in the face of the multitude, calling in vain for opponents, and then a less famous animal is brought forward, and the men come out against it at once.

There is one amusement of which the villager never tires, and that is the play. It is a great day in the hamlet when a band of actors arrives in the place. If it is a moonlight night, the rude stage will be set up by the time the villagers have had their suppers, and the play will begin about ten o'clock at night, and go on till four in the morning. The first hour of its performance is given over to the funny man, the buffoon, who makes his listeners roar with laughter at his queer antics and gestures, his jokes and stories. Then a play is given, and it is followed with close attention. At the end of each performance the players spread a cloth near the stage and invite the audience to throw money into it. While this is being done, some of the actors sing and play on musical instruments. At one corner of the cloth the buffoon is posted, and as each person throws his contribution on it, the buffoon shouts out the name of the man at the top of his voice, and says something amusing in praise of the giver. This makes the crowd laugh, and encourages others to give, and those who like to hear their generosity well spoken of will contribute three or four times, getting a louder chorus of thanks and praise each time.

The players have only a small stock of dramas—two or three well-known stories—but the villagers never tire of them. Time and again they listen to the same play, and seem at each performance to find it as fresh and attractive as ever. Here is the story of a play, of which they are very fond, the famous "Markanda":

Once there were a man and a woman who had no son, and they prayed to the great god Siva and entreated that he would bless them with a child. In answer to their prayers, Siva appeared to them, and said that he would give them a son, but they must make a choice. He would give them a son who would be beautiful, good, devoted to the gods and to learning, but must die at the age of sixteen; or he would give them a son who would be ugly, wicked, and heartless, but would live to be a hundred. "Now," said Siva, "which do you choose?"

The parents chose the good son. The child was born, and he was as beautiful as the day, and as good as gold. He was named Markanda, and he grew up strong, and brave, and handsome, and at length he gained the age of fifteen years. Now, he observed that his father and mother grew grave and unhappy, and that every day their sorrow increased. He urged them to tell him what was wrong. At first they would not, lest they should sadden the days of life which remained to him. But he pressed them, until at last he learned the cruel truth, that he had only a year to live, and that his fate was settled without hope of change, for the god Siva had decreed it.

Markanda felt very sorrowful when he heard this dreadful news, but he continued to pray to the gods, hoping that his devotion might yet save him from the fate which threatened him. As the fatal day drew near, he left his home and his parents, and went forth into the depths of the jungle, where a mighty sacred river was flowing. He bathed in the stream, and continued in this solitary place to pray without ceasing to Siva that his life might be spared, and that he should not be cut off in the flower of his days.

The day came, and the Angel of Death appeared riding on a buffalo. He shot at Markanda, and his arrows were the sharp, poisoned shafts of affliction and death. But the youth continued his earnest prayers to Siva, and his devotion

BY THE SACRED RIVER.

was such that the arrows turned aside and did him no harm. Next, the Angel of Death loosed a multitude of fiery shafts, shooting upon Markanda with all his strength, but not one inflicted a wound, nor did all the terrors of the dread angel disturb the boy for a moment from his prayers. Again the Angel of Death emptied his quiver of its most deadly arrows, and again all was in vain.

Then the Angel of Death grew furious—he who never before had known defeat—and drew his terrible sword, and advanced upon Markanda, to slay the boy with his own hand. But at this moment Siva appeared, and drove away the Angel of Death, and granted the boy his life. But the word of a god must not be broken. Siva had said that Markanda should not pass the age of sixteen, so he gave him an eternity of youth, commanding him to live for ever as a lad of sixteen!

VII

HOW THE VILLAGE IS RULED

The little community is ruled by its own officers, the chief of whom is the headman. This office descends from father to son, and the headman is a kind of perpetual mayor and magistrate of the place. He is the chief of the "Council of Five Elders," the village court known as the *panchiyat*. The village elders are elected by the people themselves, and they may belong to any class save the lowest; they are, as a rule, responsible men who have gained the respect and confidence of their fellow-villagers.

The *panchiyat* deals with all sorts of small offences and disputes. It hears complaints, arranges quarrels, and arbitrates upon all cases where the suit concerns matters up to the value of one hundred rupees. In cases of serious crime, or disputes affecting large sums, the matter goes up to the higher courts—the Government courts. But these cases rarely happen in a village. As a rule, the Council of Five Elders can easily handle and straighten out all the tangles of village life.

They deal with cases of petty theft, of misbehaviour, of fighting and quarrelling, of trespassing animals, of disputes with regard to the ownership of land, and such-like matters. If one of the village workers—the barber, the washerman, the carpenter—has not received his dues from a villager, he brings his case before the elders, and it is argued out before them. It is not often that the decision of the Council of Five Elders is disobeyed. When it is, the punishment is simple, but severe. The offender is sent to Coventry; no one is allowed to speak to him, or to have any dealings with him in any shape or form. In a community where a close social life is the rule, this punishment soon brings a disobedient man to his senses, and he is glad to carry out the decision of the Council and remove the ban from himself and his household.

When any person has a case to bring before the village court, he informs the watchman, and the latter will summon the parties before the elders. The watchman is a very important member of the hamlet. It is his duty to guard the place from thieves, and raise an alarm at night upon any sign of fires breaking out. He lies down to sleep by day, and with the dusk he is expected to be afoot, not only to patrol the village, but to watch the fields near at hand, lest thieves should plunder the crops. Sometimes he carries a spear, sometimes a great staff, which is often ten feet long. He wields this immense club with great dexterity, and cases have been known where a watchman has killed a thief with a single blow.

At the sitting of the *panchiyat* it is the watchman who brings the parties to the dispute before the judges, and he asks the person interested in the case to give him some money as security. This money is handed over to the chief judge, who holds it until the case is decided, when it is restored. The sitting is held either in a court-house belonging to the village or in the open, under a tree or beside a fountain. Very often the meeting is at night, after the work of the day is finished and the judges have had their supper, and if there is a moon, the people gather in the centre of the village in the moonlight. If it is dark, they go to the court-house, where there is a lamp so dim as scarcely to make darkness visible. But it is ample for their purposes; everything is settled by word of mouth, and if an agreement has to be drawn up in writing, that will be seen to the next day.

But in cases where people from hamlets near by are concerned, the meeting must be held by day, for no one is willing to go far from his home after darkness has fallen. Such a meeting very often presents a most striking and picturesque sight. Crowds of people of all ages and ranks swarm around the great tree under which the court is to be held. The Council of Five Elders, in their best robes, sit beneath the tree, and around them sit the spectators in close-packed rows, a mass of striking colour, with turbans and robes of every shade that the dyer's art can tint.

The cases come on one after the other. The judges listen to the evidence of the parties concerned and their witnesses. They ask shrewd questions, for they are past masters at dealing with all these difficulties of village life, and soon arrive at the heart of a matter. The spectators follow question and answer with eager interest, and roar with delight when a keen question drags the truth from an unwilling witness, or an apt retort is made. The judges always do their best to maintain peace among the villagers. If it is a quarrel between husband

and wife or among relations, they try to reconcile the parties; if the complaint is trivial, they let the offender go with a caution; if the case calls for punishment, they inflict a fine. Here is a description of the *panchiyat*, given from personal observation by a native Indian gentleman. In this case one man accuses another of striking his wife:

"When the court is opened the watchman of the village calls out for the parties to appear. The plaintiff is first summoned. When he enters the court-house, he prostrates himself before the judges. 'Get up,' says the chief judge. When the man gets up, he states his complaint. If all the parties are present, the judges go through the case, otherwise they postpone it until the following week. On hearing the complaint of the plaintiff in a petty quarrel, the judges ask him to bring his evidence. Then they hear the statement of the defendant and his witnesses. Before they sum up the case and give their judgment, they ask all those present to retire, and then they talk about the matter for some hours among themselves. When they have arrived at a conclusion, they call the parties to come in, and the chief judge delivers the judgment. If the judges find the accused to be guilty of the charge brought against him, he receives the following judgment: 'Thou scamp! bad donkey! pariah dog! Have you not got any work to do? How dare you assault this woman who has brought this charge against you! Beware! beware, you donkey! We charge you in the name of our village goddess Kali, to bring ten cocoanuts as a sacrifice for the sins referred to in this case, and, besides this, you will give three rupees to the village fund as a fine!' On hearing the judgment delivered by the chief, the offender prostrates himself before the judges saying: 'You must forgive me this time—you must forgive me this time!' Of course, this is the form of appeal he makes against their decisions. If any one of the judges thinks that the man is not in very good circumstances, he whispers to the other judges to reduce the sentence; if not, they insist upon the man paying the fine and breaking the cocoanuts to the goddess."

Sad to say, there are many villagers nowadays who are not willing to bring their disputes before this ancient and convenient court, which costs nothing. They prefer to carry their cases to one or other of the lawyers who now abound in the land, and these men fasten upon the ignorant peasant and encourage him to carry a case from court to court until he is wellnigh or entirely ruined. The Indian ryot is very fond of going to law, and it is not uncommon to hear of a small farmer spending a hundred pounds over a trifling affair worth, perhaps, a few shillings. He is so sure of winning his case that he will borrow the money to carry it on from the money-lender, and this means a loss of his land and a descent from comfort to poverty. Many a ryot has had bitter cause to rue the day when he went to a lawyer and took his case into a law-court instead of leaving it to the judgment of the *panchiyat*, the Council of Five Elders.

VIII

OFF TO THE MELA

WHAT is a *mela?* It is a great Hindu fair—a festival which draws to itself the country-folk from every side for many, many miles. In the village of which we have been speaking, there comes a morning when the people are astir long before the dawn, and the break of day sees them setting out in bands for a great *mela* to be held at a town ten miles away—a town standing on the banks of a sacred stream, and containing a great temple with the image of a famous god. This image is to be drawn through the streets in a grand procession, and every Hindu over a wide stretch of country will get to the town to-day if he can.

Off go the village folk—men, women, and children, for this is the one holiday for the women—some on foot, and some in carts. The carts, with big, creaking wheels, are drawn by bulls or buffaloes, and are covered by large hoods to keep off the fierce rays of the sun. As they draw near to the town where the *mela* is to be held, their country by-road runs into a great main road, and this is thronged by bands of people coming from other villages and hamlets, and the closer they get to the town, the thicker grow the streams of people pouring into the road at every turn of the way. At length they reach the town, and the first thing for everyone to do is to go down to the sacred river and bathe in its holy waters. There they will wash away their sins, and be fit to take part in the festival in honour of the god.

At the side of the river there is a *ghat*—a series of wide stone steps running down into the water, and the *ghat* is covered with crowds and crowds of people going and coming, sitting down to talk, bathing at the edge of the stream, many even drinking of the holy water. Here and there are seated figures engaged in prayer or wrapped in contemplation. Down the steps come the folk from our village, and many of them wear round their necks garlands of flowers purchased from the priests who sell them. The wearers of the garlands wade out into the stream and bend lower and lower until the current raises the garlands from their necks and the flowers float away on the stream. They then return to the steps and remove their dripping robes and put on dry ones they have brought with them. The wet robes will be spread out, and be dried in a very short time in the powerful sun.

As the time of the procession draws near, the crowds swarm into the city and take up their places along the sides of the principal streets. What a wonderful picture they make as they throng the way and jostle each other good-humouredly, and with broad smiles on every face! In the marvellous medley of colours in turbans and jackets, petticoats and *saris*—the robes of the women—nothing seems to strike a false note. Shades which it would seem impossible to blend under a dull sky seem here to melt one into the other under the glowing rays which pour from the marvellously blue sky overhead.

NATIVE SHOPS.

The ornaments of the women glitter till they make your eyes blink—every woman and girl has put on her best to do honour to this rare holiday—and bangles, necklets, nose-rings, anklets, bracelets, flash and shine in the sun as their wearers pass by.

There is great excitement when the sound of tom-toms announces that the procession is approaching. The tom-toms are the native drums beaten at every kind of ceremony, and their monotonous rub-a-dub-dub is one of the most familiar sounds of Indian life. Nearer come the drums, and now the onlookers begin to shout in their eagerness, and hail the god with cries of devotion. They can see the huge and splendidly decorated car on which the image is placed, high above the heads of the crowd. The car is drawn by sacred white oxen decorated with flowers, and is escorted by priests, while great numbers of devotees march before and behind. The image is that of the god Ganesa—a huge figure, having the body of a man and the head of an elephant—Ganesa, the elephant-headed god, he who can remove obstacles from the path of his worshippers and give them success in all their undertakings. Thus it is that the Hindu, ere he starts upon some new venture, makes offerings to Ganesa, and implores the aid of the powerful deity.

When the procession has passed, the rest of the day is given up to pleasure, and the merry-makers seek the fair on the outskirts of the city. Here a vast number of booths have been set up on an open stretch of plain, and all kinds of amusements are going on. Many of the little stalls are stocked with cakes or sweetmeats or pretty trinkets, to tempt the young people to spend their money.

The narrow alleys which run through the rows of booths are thronged with crowds, always merry and good-tempered, and full of fun. There is no roughness or drunkenness, and the people enjoy themselves like troops of good-natured children. There is plenty of music performed by native bands, in which are found two or three kettle-drums, beaten only on one side; a big drum beaten on both; a pair of clashing cymbals; and one or two trumpets; and with these instruments the players make a tremendous noise. Their performance sounds far from musical to the ears of Europeans, but it gives great pleasure to the villagers.

Besides the stalls of eatables and trinkets, there are many where useful articles are exposed for sale—things which the villagers can only see on some such occasion as this, and they move to and fro and compare articles and prices for a long time before they purchase such things as clothes, mats, combs, mirrors, knives, blocks of salt, and so on.

All sorts of performers and jugglers have come to the fair, and here and there are rings of people watching them as they perform their feats. There are snake-charmers who play on their pipes as the great snakes coil round their bodies or their necks. Here is a man with a sparrow on his finger. He sits down at the wayside, and the children gather round him, for they love to see the performing sparrow. The bird-tamer places the sparrow on the ground, and the little creature hops here and there, turning its wise head from side to side, and glancing at the children, but never attempting to fly away. Now its master takes a handful of beads from a fold of his robe and lays them on the ground in a little heap. Then he holds a thread dangling in the air. Up jumps the sparrow, takes the end of the thread in its claws and climbs up it nimbly like a man climbing up a rope. Up and down it goes, and next it takes a bead and slips it on the string. One after another the beads are threaded, and the little bird does its work so gaily and cleverly that the children are never tired of watching it.

There are acrobats who dance on ropes and twist their bodies into all kinds of shapes, and some of the best of these are mere children, boys and girls who roll their little bodies into balls, tie themselves into knots, and act as if their joints were made of indiarubber. A little girl will bend back until she is a perfect hoop, and with her eyelids pick up two straws set in the ground; or perhaps she performs the sword game. In this game she balances herself on the back of her head and her heels. Two swords are crossed on her chin, with their blades pointing inwards; another pair of swords is crossed under her neck. She then begins to revolve rapidly, and twists her body over the swords without touching the points. Only the greatest skill can save her from being wounded, but she never makes a mistake. There are also men who lead bears, and others who have performing monkeys.

As for the jugglers, there are many of them, and each juggler has his own audience. Some of them are so clever, and the tricks they perform are so strange, that we will speak of them again. Among the crowd pass the fakirs—the religious devotees—each with his begging bowl, in which the people lay their offerings; then there are the real beggars, one mass of sores or horribly deformed, some of them lepers, from whom all shrink in horror. But the leper is one of the boldest in demanding charity, for if he is refused, he will retaliate by cursing those who deny him, and everyone dreads a " leper's curse "; it is certain to bring the worst of ill-luck.

As sunset draws on, the throngs begin to break up, and streams pour from the city in every direction. It is a slow journey home on foot or by bullock-cart, and they must be on their way, lest night should overtake them farther on through the jungle, where the tiger will be abroad. As they go, the people talk over the incidents of the day. For weeks they have been discussing the coming of the *mela*. For weeks again they will recall everything that happened: it is the red-letter day of their year.

IX

INDIAN JUGGLERS

A TRAVELLER was one day dining at the table of a great official, when the talk turned upon the feats of Indian jugglers. The traveller had seen some tricks performed, and gave it as his opinion that the place of the performance had been prepared. An argument arose upon this, and an appeal was made to the host—a man who had spent a lifetime in India, spoke the language like a native, and was a great authority upon native life and customs.

The host shook his head. "I don't know how they are done," he replied; "I cannot explain the feats of a really good juggler. I have seen such a man perform hundreds of times, and I am certain only of one thing: the place was not prepared, and the mysterious skill of a clever performer is so great that he does not need any such aid. More, I will prove it to you. There is a family of jugglers living in the village not half a mile away. They shall come here and perform the usual feats, and I shall be glad if anyone will explain to me how the thing is done."

He gave orders to an attendant, and when the company went out to the broad verandah after dinner they found three men and a boy squatting at the end of the verandah awaiting their pleasure. Of the men, one was an old man, two middle-aged, and the boy was about ten years old. They were father, sons, and grandson, and all jugglers, for that was the family calling.

"Now," said the host to his disbelieving guest, "choose your own place for the performance, and they shall begin."

The gentleman had sat down in a large armchair, and he pointed, laughing, to the ground before him. "Here, at my feet," he said.

The host smiled and nodded, and then called out a few words in the native tongue to the jugglers. The old man at once rose and came forward, holding a flower-pot in his hands. "He is going to do the mango-tree trick," said the host, and pointed out to the old juggler the spot at which he was to perform. The old Hindu at once squatted near the feet of the guest. It was quite certain that he had nothing hidden about him, for he was almost naked. His whole clothing consisted of a turban and a waist-cloth. He emptied out a little dry earth from the pot and held it up to show that it was now quite empty. He then put the earth back, laid a mango-seed in the earth, set the pot at the feet of the watcher, threw a light cloth over it, and then drew back a distance of some three or four feet, so that he was well away from the flower-pot. In a few minutes he stretched out a long bare arm and raised the cloth. A tiny plant had thrust itself above the soil. He replaced the cloth and drew back, and all present watched him with the utmost attention, but could detect no movement on his part as he sat for a short time as still as an image. Once more he stretched out his arm and raised the cloth. The plant was beginning to put out branches, and leaves were springing. A third interval passed, and when he now raised the cloth there was a mango-tree fully two feet in height, with branches, leaves, and flowers, as complete as if growing in a garden! About twenty minutes had passed since he came forward, and the tree was real—there could be no doubt about that, for the guest handled it, and broke off branches and plucked the flowers.

The old man salaamed and retired, and his elder son, bearing a long sword, came forward, accompanied by the boy. The boy was carrying a basket. "Watch them closely," said the host; "this is the famous basket trick." The guest took the basket in his own hands and examined it carefully. It was a large basket, with a deep lid, made of common wicker-work, and the eyes of the spectators assured them that it was quite empty. The basket was set down, and the boy jumped into it. The lid was put on, but the boy seemed far too large for the basket, and the lid would not close by several inches. The man sprang on the cover and forced it down, the boy disappearing from sight little by little as the cover was driven down upon him. At last the cover was in its place, and was made fast.

The juggler stood back, and began to talk with the boy, whose answers came clearly from the basket. The answers appeared to make the man angry, for suddenly he whipped up his sword and drove it clean through the basket. There was a piercing scream from the imprisoned boy, and the sword was drawn back running with blood. But again and again it was thrust through and through the basket, and the man's anger, the shrieks of the victim, and the streaming blood, seemed so real that the guest sprang from his chair to interfere. He would have done so had not his host laid a restraining hand on his arm. Suddenly the juggler stepped back and squatted motionless before the basket. A few moments passed, and then he darted out one of his long bare legs, and gave the basket a sharp kick with his naked foot. It rolled lightly and easily to the feet of the guest. The latter opened it, and, to his astonishment, it was empty. There was no sign of the prisoner, no sign of blood. At this moment the spectators began to applaud. He looked up and saw the boy coming from the far end of the verandah, bowing and smiling as he came. But how had he got out of the basket and left the spot? That was the mystery that the onlookers could not solve.

The second son now came forward, and his performance was a simple trick, but as hard to explain as any. He asked for a small earthenware vessel, and a tray was brought from the kitchen containing a number of pots. From this tray he chose a pipkin with a spout on it, not unlike a teapot. He handed it to the guest, and the latter looked carefully at it, inside and out, and was satisfied that it was a common earthenware pot, such as is often used in native cookery. The juggler did not touch the pot again, but asked the gentleman to fill it with water and place it where he liked. This was done, and the man seated himself on the ground a dozen feet from the pipkin. In a short time he turned towards the little pot and beckoned it, at the same time chanting, *Ao! Ao!* (Come! Come!) To the wonder of all, the

A BEGGAR.

pot at once began to jump towards him, the water spilling over its side at every jump it gave. When it was about seven feet from him he ordered it to stop, and it stopped. Then he began to wave his hands in circles, and the pipkin described a complete circle round him at the word of command, finally pausing at the feet of the gentleman who had filled it, and had been the last to touch it. There the juggler left it. He rose, salaamed, and returned quietly to his companions.

The final trick was now performed by the old man, and it seemed to everyone the most wonderful of all. He came forward, just as lightly clothed as before, and holding in one hand a dried snake-skin. He offered this to the gentleman, who took it in his hands, felt it, and examined it carefully. It was a dry, shrivelled skin, which crackled beneath his fingers as he turned it over and rubbed it. He gave the skin back to the old juggler who held it out at the full length of his naked right arm for some moments. Then he began to stroke the skin gently with his left hand, keeping both bare arms at full stretch all the time. He stroked and stroked, and, to the wonder of all, it was seen that the skin was swelling with life. The dull shrivelled skin took upon it the hues it had lost, and with every movement it rounded and grew, until within ten minutes the old juggler held a large cobra writhing in his hand and winding its folds about his long thin arm. He tossed it deftly to the ground and it reared at once, hissing and darting out its forked tongue, and expanding its hood, as if eager to strike its prey. Now the elder son, who had followed his father, squatted down near the terrible deadly snake, and began to charm it, playing a soft slow air on his pipe. In a short time he had stilled the fierce reptile, and before long he secured it safely in a wicker basket. Now it could be closely examined, and all could assure themselves it was alive, and its poison fangs were untouched, and that a stroke from those gaping jaws would have meant certain death.

The host turned to the guest with a smile. "That is a good trick," he remarked. "Can you explain how it's done ? I can't." And the guest had to admit that he could not explain either, and that he was satisfied that the ground had not been prepared on this occasion.

At this moment the head-man of the village appeared, and announced that, after the family of jugglers had been summoned, a wandering fakir had arrived in the village, and now wished to display his powers. The host conversed for a few moments with the fakir, then turned to the guests and said : "He will show us the rope-trick."

The fakir called for a rope, and a strong piece of cord, such as is used to fasten goods on a country cart, was brought to him. He took it, whirled it a few times round his head, and tossed it into the air. It stood up straight and firm, as if it were hanging down from a support, though it appeared to have no support of any kind. The little boy now came forward and went up the rope nimbly hand over hand. Up and up he went, and suddenly the fakir threw the end of the rope up after him, and nothing was to be seen. For a few seconds the fakir stood motionless, then he began to climb. He rose steadily from the ground, making all the motions of a man climbing a rope, though no rope was there. On and on he went, until his form grew smaller and smaller, and he seemed to vanish into the sky. The amazed guest was still staring in wonder into the empty air, when someone said: "Hullo! here they come." He looked down, to see the fakir and the boy approaching the spot as if they had emerged from a clump of bushes fifty yards away.

"How is it done?" he gasped.

"It is some form of illusion," replied his host; "but how they produce the illusion upon us I cannot say. But I am certain they have powers we do not understand."

Nor could the guest understand it, but he had no more to say about an easy explanation of the jugglers' tricks, and he looked upon the party with deep interest as they bowed low and uttered many thanks for the rupees with which they were rewarded.

X

HOMES IN THE CITY

The homes of an Indian city are many, for the houses lie close packed along the narrow streets, and they vary from the tiny one-roomed cottage of the labourer to the fine mansion of the wealthy merchant. Of the great mass of dwellings where the working poor live there is little to be said. The single room contains mats, perhaps a native bedstead, and an array of cooking-pots—that is all. The younger children tumble about in the sun; the elder are set to some task as soon as they can earn a *pice*—which is worth one farthing—and the parents toil as coolies, bearing heavy burdens, in order to keep the wolf from the door.

In the chief streets the houses are of two or more stories, with balconies and flat roofs, where the people take the air, and often sleep when the nights are very hot. Sometimes the balconies are of woodwork, beautifully carved in quaint shapes and figures, and painted in bright colours, so that the street looks very gay in the sunshine. On the ground-floor are the shops, each like a big cupboard in the wall, with the doors thrown back. Inside the shop sits the owner. If he is a craftsman, he is hard at work at his trade, and you see him making the very goods he has to sell. If he is a trader, he squats on a rug and waits for customers, nor does he by sign or sound attempt to call upon the passers-by to examine his wares.

The street is packed with a throng of men and women, mostly bare-footed, some clad in robes of bright colours, some men wearing so little that they look like bronze statues come to life; through the crowd jostle ox-carts laden with goods, and sacred bulls wander about as calmly as if they owned the place. And so they do. The bulls which belong to a Hindu temple ramble about the streets as a pet-dog rambles about the home of his master. If the bull sees something he would like to eat in a shop, he marches in and eats it, and the dealer bows low before him. If he smells something nice in a house, in he goes and sniffs round till he finds it. No one dreams of driving him out or of refusing him the dainty. He is at once offered the best the people have, and his entrance is looked upon as an honour, and sure to bring a blessing on the house.

The homes of wealthy natives lie in a part of the town well away from the busy quarters. The houses are sometimes built close together, with only very narrow alleyways between them, and the alleys twist and wind between high walls. This makes for safety. It is not possible for large mobs to enter these winding ways, and, again, there is often a very strong door placed at the entrance of a lane, so that the people within can shut themselves up in times of disorder. From the alley the house is entered by a doorway, beautifully carved, and on the flat walls near at hand are paintings of animals or gods. The visitor enters a court around which the house is built. The men's rooms are on the ground floor, and the upper walls are pierced by windows, which are closed by latticed shutters. These windows give light and air to the zenana—the women's portion of the house—and through the slats of the shutters the ladies can peep into the court and see the coming and going of those who call at the house.

They never see visitors more nearly than that. A Hindu lady of high caste is shut up closely in the zenana, and no man save her husband ever sees her face. She very rarely leaves her apartments, but occasionally she does pay a visit to another zenana. Then she is carried in a palanquin so closely curtained that no one may peep into it, and when she leaves her own house or enters that of her friend, some of her women surround her and enfold her in a sort of small tent of muslin, so that she moves quite unseen.

The rooms on the ground floor of this dwelling may be paved, but the upper rooms have, of course, floors of wood. But the wood is not seen. It is not considered clean enough to eat from, and all Hindus use the floor as a table. So the planks are covered with earth, and the earth is finally plastered with cow-dung. This floor is very carefully swept, and the plastering renewed as it wears away.

The crowd of people in a Hindu household would seem remarkable to a Western visitor. There are a number of men, and if a lady goes into the zenana, she finds a large number of women and swarms of children tumbling about. The reason is simple. The Hindu son does not set up a house for himself when he marries. He stays on at home, and, as every Hindu marries, there are as many families as there are sons, all under the one roof.

Where are the Hindu daughters ? There is not one over twelve years of age to be found in the house. They have all been married and gone to other homes. It is the custom among the Hindus for all girls to be married at an early age, and, as a rule, by the age of twelve every girl is a wife or a widow. The Hindu father and mother consider it a most sacred duty to see that every daughter is married, and to be sure that this shall happen, they betroth and marry children, even sometimes babies in the cradle. Many a little girl is fetched from her play at three or four years of age and made to go through a marriage ceremony. When it is over, she returns to her doll, and years pass before she is sent to her husband's home.

She may, perhaps, be ten or eleven when this occurs, and her future happiness depends entirely upon what kind of people she goes among. She can never hope for any more help or comfort from her own father and mother. She is now completely cut off from her childhood's home, and is altogether in the hands of her husband and his friends. She goes into the zenana of the new abode, and finds it ruled by the oldest woman there—her husband's mother, or, if he is a boy much of her own age, perhaps his grandmother. Then there may be a bevy of other women, wives of other sons of the house. If the old lady at the head of affairs is kind and good-hearted, all goes well for the little bride, but if she is cruel and the other women are unkind, there is no one to help the unlucky child.

Sometimes she is treated with great cruelty—beaten, half-starved, made to do the roughest and hardest work. But she has no hope of escape, and no hope of assistance. It is of no use for her to think of running back to her parents; they would not take her in. If she left her husband's home, it would bring great disgrace upon her father; it would cause him to lose caste, so he will not support her in the smallest degree against her husband's family. Mrs. Fuller gives an example of an unlucky child-marriage, which would stand for many others. She says:

"The girl's appearance did not suit the young husband, and if she went near him to serve him with food, he would hit her on the crown of her head with his knuckles. Though she was but ten years old, they expected her to do every kind of work. She did the household work, brought water for all, cleaned the utensils and the floor, did the washing, milked the cow, and kept its stable clean. If the cow did not yield the proper quantity of milk, she was punished. Her father-in-law would hang her up to the beam of the roof and beat her pitilessly. He would sometimes suspend her to the same place by the ankles, and under her head, thus suspended, place a vessel with red-hot coals, on which he sprinkled red pepper to almost suffocate her. Sometimes when he had hung her to the rope, for fear she should be tempted to break the rope and fall, he would lay branches of prickly pear on the floor beneath her. When her father heard of all this cruelty, he exhorted her not to run away, but to stay and die."

Sometimes a little girl is a widow: the boy or man to

whom she has been married has died before she became old enough to be sent to her husband's home. The fate of all Hindu widows is a very sad one. A Hindu girl or woman of good caste may not marry again, and she is treated in a very harsh and unkind fashion. The Hindu widow has her head shaved at once upon her husband's death, she is clad on that day and for all days afterwards in the meanest and coarsest garments; she is only allowed to eat one meal a day, and upon two days in each month she does not get even that single meal; she has to strip off all her ornaments and jewels; she may never attend any festivity or merry-making; and if she went near any joyful meeting, she would be at once driven away, for her mere presence is regarded as bringing the worst of ill-luck. No one will eat or drink food or water upon which her shadow has fallen, for it is looked upon as unclean. If a man, upon starting a journey, catches sight of a widow, he will turn back; he has seen a thing of ill-omen, and the journey would have an unlucky ending.

The saddest fate is that of children who have never known anything save widowhood. A girl is married as a mere infant; her husband dies while she is very young. The child knows little or nothing about it, and only understands in a very vague manner what it all means. She plays about as merrily as ever, for she will not be called upon to enter the state of widowhood until she reaches the age at which she is sent to her husband's house. It is true she gets a foretaste of her future state if she should wander near a wedding-feast or some such merry-making. She is driven away as a sight of evil.

When she reaches the age of ten or eleven, her head is shaved, she is dressed in the coarse *sari*, the single garment of widowhood, and she is exposed to the insults and abuse of her husband's friends. The latter show the greatest ill-will against her. They believe that in some former life she has committed a great sin, and this has brought upon her the curse of widowhood in her present existence. The Hindu religion teaches that souls return to this earth for life after life in various bodies, and that a sin committed in some former existence may bring punishment in the new life. The friends of the husband say that it was the fate of this child to become a widow, and because of that her husband died. Had he married someone of a better fate, he would have lived.

In the old days widows used to commit *suttee*—that is, they were burned alive in company with the husband's dead body. Hindus do not bury their dead. The bodies are placed on a great pile of wood and burned to ashes. But the British Government put down *suttee*, and also made it lawful for widows to remarry. Yet, so strong is custom among the natives, that, though there are many millions of Hindu widows, only a score or so of them are remarried in a year.

XI

FROM BIRTH TO MARRIAGE

When a baby is born in a Hindu home, it will be received very gladly if it is a boy; the parents rejoice because the gods have given them a son. If the father is rich, he will show his pleasure by making a splendid feast for the priests and his friends. All the beggars in the country-side will flock to the house, for they know well that the wealthy man will distribute food and money among them, that all may rejoice with him on the birth of his son.

If it is a daughter, there is quite another face on things. The mother is sad, the friends shake their heads as if sorry for the misfortune which has befallen the house, and the father thinks that the gods are angry with him because they have sent him a daughter. This seems very wrong and unreasonable to us, but the causes must be sought in the views of the Hindus and their way of life. In the first place, a Hindu believes that after his death he cannot be happy in the next world unless his son has performed certain rites and ceremonies on his behalf. A daughter cannot do this, so he earnestly wishes for a son. In the second place, a son is a son always—the prop and support of the house. He will never leave his parents, but their home will be his home until the day of his death. But a daughter is a daughter only for a very few years; she will marry and go to her husband's house, and thenceforth she has neither share nor part in the home in which she was born. Whatever the need of her parents may be, she cannot tend or aid them : she belongs entirely to her husband's family. Among the higher castes the separation is so complete that a father may not visit his married daughter's home, and a man has been heard to boast that he had not even drunk water from the well of the village in which his married daughter lived.

In the third place, there is the question of the dowry. The Hindu husband often expects to receive a large sum of money with his wife; so that if there are many daughters of a house the parents are pinched to provide dowries. And we must remember that every daughter must be married. Nothing would more horrify Hindu parents than the idea that a daughter might remain unmarried at the age of fourteen. It is against every custom of their life, and custom is a tyrant in India.

Upon these scores, then, daughters are, as a rule, unwelcome—so unwelcome that, in the old days, they were often put to death. When a father heard that a daughter was born, he said nothing, but raised his hand, with the thumb clasped round the fingers. The sign meant that it was not to live, and the child was killed. The British Government set to work to stop this crime, and it is no longer done openly. But it is said that in some parts of the country it still goes on in secret, and it may easily be so, for the law stops short on the threshold of the zenana, where no man may be admitted save the master of the house.

When a child is born one of the first things done is to

fetch the fortune-teller. He comes and looks very carefully at the marks on the baby's head. These are the lines between the bones of the skull, such as all children show. But the Hindus believe that in these marks the fate of the child can be read, and this very old story is told about them :

Long, long ago a daughter was born to the great god Brahma, the creator of all things, and his wife begged that he would tell her the fate of their child. Brahma was seated with his back towards his wife and the infant, but he stretched out his hand behind him towards the child. In his hand he held a pen of gold, and with this pen he wrote on the infant's head. He could not see the letters he was forming, but his wife could, and she cried out in alarm, for she saw that a dreadful fate was promised for her child. She called upon Brahma to change the writing at once. He did so, but her terror increased, for this fate was worse than the last. Again she begged him not to leave so cruel a fate on the head of their daughter. Brahma wrote a third time, but now he did not give his wife a chance to urge him anew. Before she could say a word, he hurled his golden pen far from him, and since that day he has never written but once on the head of each child ; so that when a child is born the fortune-teller is called in, and he pores over those markings in the tiny skull, and calls them the writings of Brahma. In those writings it is believed that the child's fate is set down, and the parents listen with great eagerness and anxiety as the fortune-teller prophesies what will happen to their little one.

For the first few years of a child's life he is allowed to

tumble about and play just as he fancies, nor is any attention paid to what he says or does, for he is regarded as having no soul until he has attained the age of seven years. At about eight or nine years he is considered old enough to enter his caste, and this entrance is conducted, in the case of a high-caste boy, with many ceremonies. He now puts on the sacred thread which is the mark of his caste. He wears it over his right shoulder, and from the moment he puts it on he must obey every caste rule. The priest who puts the thread on him for the first time also whispers in his ear the *mantra*—the sacred text or saying of his family. This *mantra* he must repeat every morning and evening, and he must always bathe before he tastes food. Besides the sacred thread, he is shown how to paint his caste marks on his face and body. There are many marks for the different castes, and a Hindu has only to glance at the mark on a man's forehead to know at once to what caste he belongs.

Ere long the day of his marriage arrives, and marriage is the greatest event in the life of a native. His wedding is celebrated, not only as well as he or his parents can afford, but often in a style which is absurd when the means of the family are considered. Friends and relations are invited from far and near ; splendid dinners are spread ; the priests are feasted and receive rich presents ; musicians and dancing-girls are hired, at great expense, to amuse the guests ; the poor crowd to the place and clamour for gifts, which must be provided ; horses and palanquins are obtained ; fine robes and ornaments are bought ; and the day often closes with a magnificent exhibition of fireworks.

All this means money, and a great deal of money. It must be done, for custom demands it. How is the money found if the people are not well off ? By loading their land with mortgages, or by borrowing from the money-lender. It is a very common thing to discover that a family has been utterly crippled for years by a wedding ; it is left staggering under a load of debt, and if it gets into the hands of a grasping money-lender, that often leads to utter ruin.

The wedding-day is the day of her life to the bride. Hitherto she has been merely a daughter, and looked upon as a sort of encumbrance ; for the future she will be a wife and retire to the seclusion of the zenana. But for that day she is in the centre of the stage, the observed of all observers. She wears a splendid dress of scarlet. If her family is wealthy, her robe is shot with gold and flashes with gems ; if her station is humble, it glitters almost as brightly with tinsel.

The ceremony of marriage is performed in many different ways in different parts of India, but certain rites are found everywhere. The chief of these rites are three in number. First, the pouring of rice or wheat, according to the district, over the heads of the bridal pair. This is done to bring good luck, and to obtain a blessing on the union. This custom has passed from India to Europe, and it is a common thing in our own country to throw rice after or over a wedded pair for good luck. Second, the bride is received into her husband's family, for in future she will belong to it entirely. This is carried out by the solemn eating of food by the bridal pair from the same dish. When this is over, the bride's forehead is marked with scarlet, the symbol which shows that she is a married woman. In former times the mark was made with blood drawn from both, but now it is painted. The third rite—that of the sacred fire—is very ancient and of great importance, for it is considered to be the binding rite of the marriage. A fire is solemnly lighted by the priest, and bride and bridegroom step seven times round it. It is a survival of early forms of fire-worship, and as the hearth fire is supposed to stand for the home, so the moving of the bride and bridegroom round the sacred fire is supposed to bind them closely together in the service of the home.

A MINSTRELS' BALCONY.

XII

THE HOME OF THE RAJAH

THE Rajah, the Indian Prince, has a palace, just as the ryot has a hut. But without the ryot there would be no Rajah, for the latter maintains his princely state upon the revenues which spring from the labour of the peasants who till the soil of his kingdom. There are many Rajahs in India—nearly a thousand of them—for the land is full of native states, large and small. The chief of these rulers are very great Princes indeed, and their provinces are as large as some European countries; but at the bottom of the scale are Rajahs of very slight consequence. A well-known writer on India, speaking of the smaller Rajahs, remarks:

"One I knew would hobnob with my servants, and his revenue from his hereditary kingdom was considerably less than £200 a year. He lived in a most picturesque old castle, inhabited chiefly by snakes, scorpions, and bats; but he spent most of his life in the neighbouring British law-court, defending actions for debt. I remember entering a walled town in Kattywar and seeing what looked like a loafer drinking spirits out of a bottle as he squatted in the gateway. 'Who are you?' I asked. 'The King of this country,' he replied, with perfect truth.

He boasted an ancestry that was supposed to go back to the sun."

There are no grander homes in the world than the palaces in which the great Rajahs live. Such a palace may stand on a ridge of the hills, or on a broad stretch of sun-baked plain, or beside a great stream; but it is built of the most costly materials, and finished with great beauty of workmanship. You enter such a palace by a magnificent gateway leading into a great courtyard, and from the courtyard the halls of audience may be gained. These halls, where the Rajah sits in state to receive his visitors, are vast apartments, often open on one or two sides, and walls and floors are of great slabs of pure white marble, often inlaid in rich and delicate colours. In the walls are set pierced marble screens framed in jasper, agate, lapis lazuli, and other precious stones, and the open sides are guarded by balustrades of marble wrought into patterns so delicate that they seem like lace-work.

Within are the private rooms of the palace, spacious, so that they may be as cool as possible in the terrible heat of the Indian summer, and in the marble floors there are often channels cut, so that water may flow through the palace in times of the greatest heat, and help to cool the air. The women's apartments—the zenana—lie together at one corner of the great building, and are most strictly and jealously shut off from the rooms to which men may be admitted. Lovely gardens spread round the palace, and the garden nearest to the zenana may be walled in for the use of the Rajah's women-folk; but in some of the stricter Hindu palaces the women never leave the shelter of the zenana walls.

The Home of the Rajah

The rooms of the palace which are furnished in native fashion look simple and bare to Western eyes. The floors may be covered with handsome mats and carpets, and there are piles of cushions for the Rajah and his friends to sit upon, with their legs tucked under them. There are also small tables, beautifully carved and gilded, upon which pipes and cups are placed; but of furniture in the usual sense of the word there is very little. But many Rajahs have a number of their apartments filled with English furniture, and in these they receive their European guests. A Rajah who has travelled and spent much time abroad will have this furniture set in proper order, but a ruler who has been little outside his own State often arranges things in a very odd fashion.

One writer, who had a letter of introduction to a Rajah who dwelt in a distant corner of the Indian Empire, speaks of being received in a room which his host fondly believed to resemble an English sitting-room. It was a huge apartment, crammed from end to end with furniture from Tottenham Court Road. In one corner stood a massive brass bedstead; on it there was no bed, but at least a score of clocks, all ticking away, and telling all sorts of time. Of these clocks some were of fine workmanship, some of the cheapest make. Scattered about the spacious floor, higgledy-piggledy, without the slightest semblance of order, were tables, chairs, and sofas of all sizes and qualities, while dozens of mirrors were fastened on the walls, and a huge hat-rack occupied a place of honour in the middle of the room. There was a great library-table, covered with morocco leather, and carefully set on the broad surface were half a dozen towel-rails; and when the visitor was offered a seat, he found it was a cheap cane-bottomed bedroom chair. Every article was coated with dust and dirt.

But, you may ask, where was the Rajah's wife, and had the lady no better idea how to arrange her house? She was in the zenana, and had never been out of it since the day of her marriage. The Rajah belonged to the strictest caste of Hindus, and his wife had never seen the furniture, had never even set foot in the room where it stood.

Over this small city of chambers, corridors, pavilions, baths, and gardens, the Rajah reigns absolute; but his power in the country round about is not so great as it was before the British Government was set up in India. In the old days he was an autocrat, and the life and wealth of every man in his State was at his mercy. Now the power of life and death does not rest in his hands, nor may he seize the property of his subjects. At the Court of every native ruler there is a British Resident, who keeps an eye on the manner in which the Rajah rules, and who does not permit him to interfere in matters outside his own kingdom.

Still, a Rajah has immense power among his own people, and his influence for good or ill is very great. A Rajah who is enlightened and progressive can raise his people as none other can. They will learn from him and follow him as they would follow no other man. And a Rajah who is ignorant and backward can keep his people back in like fashion to himself. The poorest ryot has a sympathy with his lord and master. He is as proud of the Rajah's magnificence as if it were his own. When the Prince rides out in a golden howdah set on an elephant, whose splendid trappings of gold brocade glitter with gems, the ryot does not compare the Rajah's pride with his own poverty, and reflect that it is from his toil that this glory springs, like a lily from a mudbank. The peasant is deeply interested in his lord's train of richly dressed horsemen, of retainers in silks and jewels, of attendants and servants. And if the Rajah does not "squeeze" his ryots too heavily in the way of taxes, he is regarded with respect and devotion.

At the Court of the Rajah are many officials, such as his Ministers of State and the officers of his army, and among his attendants are some that would seem strange to us. For instance, there is the Court Astrologer—a wise man, who reads the stars, and casts horoscopes, and gives advice as to future events. All Hindus, high and low, are fond of consulting astrologers and fortune-tellers, and nothing is done until a fortune-teller has picked out a lucky day for the action. He is consulted as to whether a marriage will be prosperous; whether a purchase or a sale will be favourable to the buyer or seller; how the verdict will go in a lawsuit; how an illness will turn out; when will be a favourable time to betroth a son or daughter; or how long the inquirer will live.

The last is a very favourite question, and in connection with it, a story is told of a Rajah who had a very famous astrologer at his Court. One day the Rajah asked the astrologer: "How long shall I live?" "My lord, I must consult the stars," he replied. He did so, and returned. "Oh, my lord," said he, "you will live for two years."

The Rajah was aghast. "Only two years?" he cried. "Not more," replied the astrologer. The Rajah trembled, and his face became sad. Now, the Prime Minister was attending upon his master, and he stepped forward.

"Oh, my lord," said he, "be not uneasy. This man speaks foolishness."

"Who can prove that?" murmured the Rajah.

"I can," said the Prime Minister; and he turned to the astrologer.

"Hast thou consulted the stars for thyself?" asked the Prime Minister. "Knowest thou the length of thy days?"

"I do," replied the astrologer boldly; "and I shall yet live for twenty-three years."

The words were scarce out of the astrologer's mouth when the Prime Minister whipped his broad scimitar from its sheath. With a single stroke of the keen curved blade he swept the astrologer's head from his shoulders. Then he pointed to the body with his dripping blade.

"Oh, my lord," said he, "could a man who knew not how near was the hour of his own death tell you truly how near was the hour of yours? Take comfort. Did I not say that he spoke foolishness?"

Then the Rajah was easy in mind once more, and praised his clever Minister, and gave him a robe of honour and many rich presents.

Yet, though Hindus may tell stories like these, they do not act up to them, but give the predictions of the fortune-teller a great place in their minds, and follow the directions of the astrologers as to lucky and unlucky days with the closest care.

Another officer is the falconer, for falconry was the old royal sport of India, and many Rajahs are still attended by the falconers bearing the keen-eyed hawks on the wrist or on a frame. The birds are loosed beside the marsh, or river, or lake, where they strike down teal and wild-ducks, or on the open plain, where they find partridge or quail. But a well-trained hawk will not strike a bird when flying over water, for it understands the danger of falling with its prey and being drowned.

Many a Rajah lives, as it were, a double life. In his palace he is a great Indian ruler, clothed in rich silken robes, with a great muslin turban on his head, a scimitar at his side, and slippers on his feet. He rides out on a war-horse or an elephant, and is attended by a train of retainers, who are dressed and armed as the retainers of his house have been dressed and armed for centuries. His subjects bend to the ground before him, and to the English on-looker the conditions of his life seem to belong to old romance and the days of the Arabian Nights. But when he wants a holiday, he slips off to London or Paris, and appears there as a brown-faced gentleman, clad in the most correct form of European dress, and not to be distinguished, save by the shade of his skin, from any other man about town.

If, however, he belongs to one of the higher castes, this crossing of the sea—the " Black Water," as the Hindus call it—will give him much trouble when he reaches home again. For the crossing of the Black Water throws a man out of caste, and caste is more powerful than any

Rajah. To put himself right again, he must submit himself to the priests and undergo a process of purification. In this process the cow takes a foremost place, for she is the sacred animal of the Hindus, and it is believed that she can free the Hindu from sin. The out-of-caste man must not only bathe in water which has been mixed with milk and cow-dung, but he must also drink some of the compound, and when he has done this, and made a splendid feast for the brethren of his caste, and given great fees to the Brahmin priests, he is once more in caste and easy in his mind.

THE RAJAH'S ELEPHANT.

XIII

HOMES OF THE WILD FOLK

In the depths of the Indian jungle and among the hills there still exist wild tribes whose members are little or no better than savages.

Some of these tribes are believed to be the ancient inhabitants of the land—the old, old stock which lived in India before a Hindu or a Moslem had crossed the barrier of the Himalayas. Among them are found the simplest and rudest kind of dwellings, and some construct no dwelling at all, but creep into caves and take shelter in holes in the rocks from night and storm.

Many of these wild primitive tribes are found in Southern India, and a tribe called the "Juangs" build about the smallest huts that human beings ever set up and called dwellings. The hut of a Juang measures about six feet wide by eight feet long, and is never tall enough for a man to stand upright in. The door is so tiny that it is a wonder how the inmates can get in at all, even on all fours. Yet, scanty as is the space within, a partition cuts the hut into two divisions. Of these, one is used as a storehouse, the other as the sole living apartment. Into the latter, not much bigger than a good-sized dog-kennel, the members of the family, with the exception of the boys, pack themselves to sleep. The boys have a little hut to themselves.

The Todas, a tribe of the Neilgherry Hills, live in a village which is known as a *Mund*. A Toda *Mund* is a collection of a few huts inside a loose stone wall, and the houses are bigger than those of the Juangs certainly, but still of no great size. The hut of a Toda is about twelve feet long and ten feet high. He builds it of bamboos set closely side by side, and their tops tied together with rattan. He plasters the bamboo walls with mud, and covers the whole with thatch, so that it looks in shape like a great waggon-tilt set on the ground. The ends are filled up with logs and plastered over, so that the building is substantial and water-tight. There is only one opening in the whole structure—a tiny hole at one end, barely two feet square. This hole serves as door, window, and chimney. A stranger wonders how the people get in or out until he sees a man or woman go flat on the ground, and wriggle his or her way in, like an eel slipping under a stone. Bold explorers who have crawled into the dark interior report that along one side there is a fixed low platform covered with skins. This is the family sleeping-place, and is the sole furnishing of the hut. But no one cares to stay long in a Toda dwelling; it is too close and dirty to be pleasant.

The Todas themselves are, in contrast to most primitive tribes, a fine-looking people—tall, well-formed, and many of the women are handsome. Their sole garment is a blanket, and as the Todas never wash either themselves or their blankets, the latter are very dirty. The ornaments of the women are big, heavy bangles made of brass or lead, and cowrie-shells strung into tassels, which are hung on necklaces of thread, the latter woven of hair or silver, according to the wealth of the wearer. A Toda never does any work save watch his buffaloes, and these he worships as the source of his food and livelihood. The operation of milking is regarded as sacred, and only the village priest is allowed to perform it. The milk is set in a dairy, and this is looked upon as a sacred spot, and no woman is allowed to enter it. When the herd of buffaloes is driven home at night, the priest and the people bend low before it, and this is their chief act of worship. They have one prayer: "May all be well; may the buffaloes be well."

The Kuravans build for themselves round huts of basket-work. They make these huts so light that a man can lift one, and when a Kuravan takes a fancy to move house, he does so in literal fact. He marches off to the new spot with his hut on his head, while his wife follows, laden with their few belongings.

The gipsy tribes use very slight shelters, though they may stay at one spot for some time. When a tribe pitches on a place where they intend to encamp, the men cut some bamboo-poles and drive them into the earth. Some slighter poles form the roof. Palm leaves are used to cover the walls and thatch the roof, and in a very short time a little village of huts has been run up—huts which will give complete shelter from the severest rains.

The bamboo is the stand-by of all the wild tribes who build simple houses, and the hill-men, above all, make full use of it. As one writer remarks of the hill-man: "He builds his house of the bamboo; he fertilizes the fields with its ashes; of its stem he makes vessels in which to carry water; with two bits of bamboo he can produce fire; its young and delicate shoots provide a dainty dinner-dish; and he weaves his sleeping-mat of fine slips thereof; the instruments with which his women weave their cotton are of bamboo. He makes drinking-cups of it, and his head at night rests on a bamboo pillow; his forts are built of it; he catches fish, makes baskets and tools, and thatches his house with the help of the bamboo. He smokes from a pipe of bamboo; and from the bamboo ashes he obtains potash. Finally, his funeral-pile is lighted with bamboo. The hill-man would die without bamboo, and the thing he finds hardest to believe is that in other countries the bamboo does not grow, and that men live in ignorance of it. Throughout the whole of India, indeed, the bamboo occupies the foremost place in the domestic economy of the inhabitants."

The gipsies catch birds very cleverly with bamboo-rods. They take a set of bamboos of differing sizes, so that each length fits into the one below, like the joints of a fishing-rod. The end of the top joint is smeared with bird-lime. When the gipsy has marked a bird sitting on a bough, he steals along very carefully till he is below it. Then he raises the rod and passes it up through the branches of the tree. He adds joint after joint until the end is near to the bird. With a swift motion he thrusts the smeared point against the feathers of the bird and secures it. The skill with which he slips the rod through the tree without making the slightest rustle or movement of a leaf is wonderful.

Some of the wildest tribes of India live among the

thick jungles which fringe the foot of the Himalayas. The Rajis are people who never leave the forest wilds. Their homes are the simplest form of shelter—small huts built of sticks and leaves—and they never stay in one spot for a long time. They ramble through the dense jungle, searching for the herbs and fruits upon which they live. Their only industry is the making of wooden bowls, and these they exchange with the villagers who dwell on the border of the jungle for grain or a little cooked food. If they have any grain or food to spare, they hide it in a hole in the rocks, or bind it up in leaves and hang it to a branch of a tree.

In the Terai—that tract at the foot of the Himalayas where the down-rushing rivers form a great and deadly swamp—live the Tharus. They are first-rate hunters, and they suffer so little from the terrible swamp-fever which haunts the Terai that some people believe the fever cannot touch them. This is not so. The Tharus largely escape because they understand very well that the fever lurks in the thick mist which lies on the sodden earth ; so, in order to escape it they raise their houses high above the ground. The first piece of work in building a Tharus village is the raising of a platform on lofty posts. On this platform they build their huts, and another precaution they take is to clear away the jungle for some distance around their dwellings.

There are some tribes among these jungle folk of whom very little is known. They are so shy and hide themselves so carefully in their wild retreats that British officers have been unable to come in close touch with them. All that can be said of them is that their homes are as simple as the nests of birds or the dens of beasts; they clothe themselves with leaves, when they wear clothing, and they live on jungle fruits and wild honey. Among many of these tribes the custom prevails of wearing ear ornaments so heavy that the lobe of the ear is greatly distended, and so large a hole is drawn out that a man could put his arm through it.

Finally, there are few tribes so wild as the people who inhabit the Andaman and Nicobar Islands in the Bay of Bengal. In 1857 a great convict settlement was formed in the South Andaman, and for some years the authorities had much trouble with the natives, but in time peace was made. But until lately it was a very dangerous business to land on the islands except at the point under British influence, for the natives were savage and bloodthirsty. The native houses look just like huge bee-hives set up on tall poles, for they are built near the shores on trunks driven into the sand. A platform is built on the posts, and this platform is sheltered by a cone-shaped structure of sticks and thatch, and entrance to the house is gained by a ladder. In this way they make themselves safe from enemies and wild beasts.

In front of the houses they set up very tall thin poles, much higher than the roof, and these poles are decked at intervals of several feet with large bunches of grass. The poles sway in the sea-breeze, and the tufts of grass flutter steadily. The natives declare that these movements will frighten away the evil spirits, of whom they stand in great fear. Another mode of scaring the demons from their huts consists in placing before the door a grotesque figure, carved and painted till it looks a most fantastic and horrible sight. Food is placed before this figure, and soon disappears. As a rule, a rambling dog or pig has made short work of it, but the native is quite satisfied if the food goes. He considers that the "scare-demon" has accepted the offering, and will continue to protect his hut.